HAPPY FOURTH OF JULY

Find our books at Amazon, Barnes & Nobles, Walmart, Books-A-Million, OverDrive, Kobo, Lulu and more!

Like, Share and Follow us on Facebook, Instagram, Twitter, Pinterest, YouTube, LinkedIn, Spotify, Apple Podcast and more!

www.SlothDreamsBooks.com

WHAT IS 4TH OF JULY?

What is...

4TH OF July

WRITTEN &
ILLUSTRATED BY
KERIANNE JELINEK

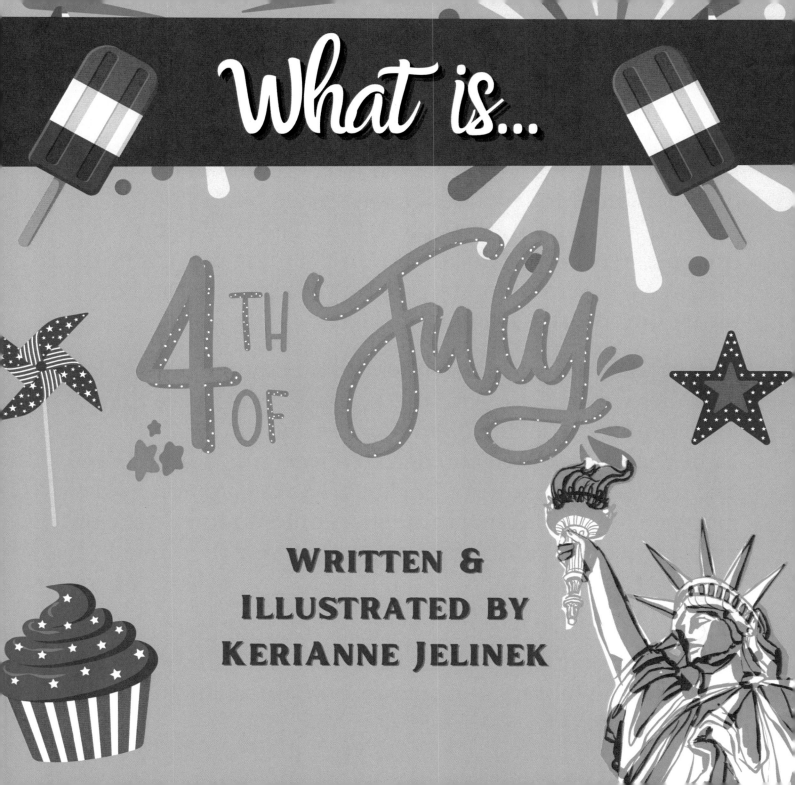

WHAT IS 4TH OF JULY?

The 4th of July is a very special holiday for Americans. The holiday is often called Independence Day and is celebrated on July 4th of every year. The holiday remembers when the Declaration of Independence was signed on July 2, 1776, and ratified two days later on July 4, 1776. The Declaration of Independence was a document proclaiming that the thirteen original colonies would be free from British rule and the Kingdom of Great Britain (England).

The Declaration of Independence said that the thirteen colonies would be free to rule, regulate and govern their own country. The document was created during the American Revolution and declared freedom from war and the overpowering rule of England. The declaration made it possible for the original thirteen colonies to form their own government. It was the first step in forming the United States of America.

Thomas Jefferson wrote the original draft of the Declaration of Independence. The original document is preserved and stored at the Library of Congress on Capital Hill in Washington, D.C.

The *Founding Fathers* were the leaders of the American Revolution who led and pushed for freedom from Great Britain. 56 of those Founding Fathers signed the Declaration of Independence. Benjamin Franklin, George Washington, John Adams, James Madison, John Jay, Alexander Hamilton, and Thomas Jefferson were the most notable founders.

On July 4, 1776, over 246 years ago, we gained our freedom to become a self-governed democratic country. Although the original declaration was intended for the thirteen colonies, we now are a country of fifty states and territories. All fifty states make up the great country of the United States of America.

On the 4th of July, people around America celebrate our freedoms. People travel, go to the beach, go boating, eat delicious foods, do barbeques, light fireworks, or do other special things to celebrate the holiday.

July the 4th will always be a special day to celebrate our country. To many people, it is a special day to show pride for being an American. Happy 4th of July!

What can you do to observe, celebrate and honor America on the 4th of July?

You can fly the American flag on your house or other safe place in honor of your country.

You can go celebrate by watching fireworks at a local venue or buy some fireworks to do at home with your family.

You can wear a fun and patriotic outfit with red, white and blue!

You can go to a local 4th of July parade. Parades are fun, festive, and celebrate our independence!

You can dress up your pet in a silly and cute patriotic costume.

You can help cook and eat a delicious BBQ. Hot dogs, hamburgers, chips, soda, and watermelon are popular choices.

You can help cook a delicious
BBQ with the help of an adult.

You can celebrate by making homemade ice cream or buying ice cream cones or festive red, white and blue popsicles.

You can help bake a yummy patriotic cake or cupcakes to share.

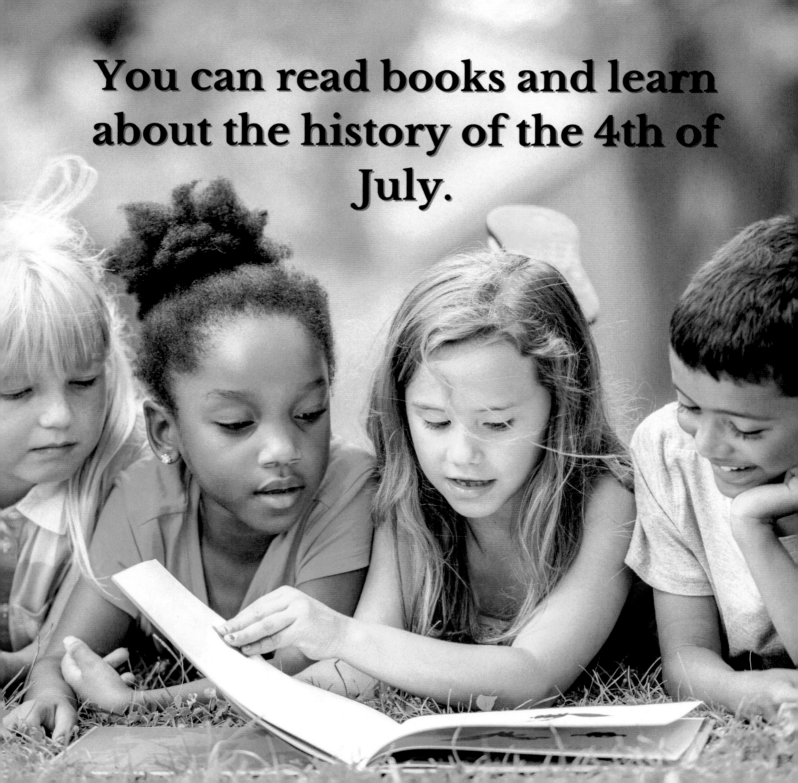

You can read books and learn about the history of the 4th of July.

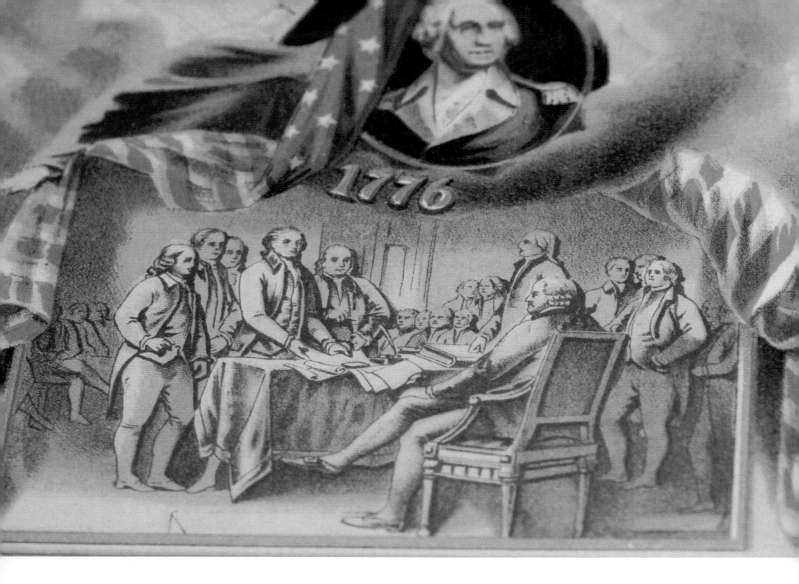

You can ask an adult or teacher to help you read the Declaration of Independence.

You can recite and learn about the Pledge of Allegiance.

I Pledge Allegiance To The Flag Of The United States Of America And To The Republic For Which It Stands One Nation Under God Indivisible With Liberty And Justice For All

You can plan a special camping trip, vacation or day at the beach to celebrate your beautiful country.

You can go boating or swimming at the lake or ocean.

You can visit a national monument and pay your respects to the Founding Fathers and all the people that worked tirelessly to see our nation become the great country of the United States of America.

IN THIS TEMPLE
AS IN THE HEARTS OF THE PEOPLE
FOR WHOM HE SAVED THE UNION
THE MEMORY OF ABRAHAM LINCOLN
IS ENSHRINED FOREVER

You can go to New York City to visit the great symbol of hope and freedom, the Statue of Liberty.

On this special day, may you feel proud to be an American. Americans are strong, resilient, dedicated, and patriotic to their country.

You can feel proud of your heritage and the diversity of people within your country. Every race, religion, creed, color and orientation is what makes America great.

May you never forget the freedoms we enjoy today, are because of the men and women that fought for all Americans to be free.

May you always remember that America is a great country because of every single person within it, including YOU!
Happy 4th of July!

HAPPY

4TH OF JULY